W9-CIH-601

DISCARD

Sports Illustrated KIDS

The Best of EVERYTHING

BASEBALL

BOOK

by Nate LeBoutillier

B4 T

11/13

J
796.35
L

CAPSTONE PRESS
a capstone imprint

Sports Illustrated KIDS books are published by Capstone Press,
1710 Roe Crest Drive, North Mankato, Minnesota 56003.
www.capstonepub.com

Copyright © 2011 by Capstone Press, a Capstone imprint.
All rights reserved.
No part of this publication may be reproduced in whole or in part, or stored in
a retrieval system, or transmitted in any form or by any means, electronic, mechanical,
photocopying, recording, or otherwise, without written permission of the publisher.
For information regarding permission, write to Capstone Press,
1710 Roe Crest Drive, North Mankato, Minnesota 56003.

 Books published by Capstone Press are manufactured with paper
containing at least 10 percent post-consumer waste.

Library of Congress Cataloging-in-Publication Data
LeBoutillier, Nate.
  The best of everything baseball book / by Nate LeBoutillier.
    p. cm.—(All-time best of sports. Sports Illustrated kids)
  Includes bibliographical references and index.
  ISBN 978-1-4296-5467-8 (library binding)
  ISBN 978-1-4296-6288-8 (paperback)
  1. Baseball—Miscellanea—Juvenile literature. 2. Baseball—Records—Juvenile literature.
  3. Baseball—Biography—Juvenile literature. I. Title. II. Series.
  GV877.L32 2011
  796.357—dc22   2010038474

Editorial Credits
Anthony Wacholtz, editor; Tracy Davies, designer;
Eric Gohl, photo researcher; Eric Manske, production specialist

Photo Credits
Dreamstime/Frank Romeo, 55 (b)
Getty Images Inc./NY Daily News Archive, 38 (all)
Jill Kalz, 36
Library of Congress, 6, 7 (all), 11 (b), 12 (all), 13 (all), 16 (all), 29 (t), 34 (b), 35 (b), 39, 41 (t), 46 (b), 50,
    52 (b), 53 (all), 60 (t)
Newscom/Icon SMI 800/Sporting News Archives, 33 (t); Ray Gora, 22 (t); SportsChrome, 33 (b)
Shutterstock/Ben Haslam, 9 (batter's box); CLM, cover (baseball), 1; Ken Inness, 57; Nicholas Piccillo,
    8–9 (helmets); Paul Brennan, cover (background); Sanderson Design, 8–9 (field)
Sports Illustrated/Al Tielemans, 10, 19 (tr), 21 (b), 31 (b), 47 (b), 59 (l & br); Andy Hayt, 34 (t); Chuck
    Solomon, 19 (br), 21 (t), 26 (b); Damian Strohmeyer, cover (bl & br), 18 (m), 46 (t), 54 (b), 59 (tr);
    David E. Klutho, cover (tl & bm), 18 (b), 49 (t), 51, 58 (t); Heinz Kluetmeier, 45, 48 (b), 49 (b); Hy
    Peskin, 17 (t); John Biever, cover (bml & bmr), 4–5, 15, 18 (t), 19 (bl), 20 (t), 54 (t); John D. Hanlon,
    32; John G. Zimmerman, 25 (all), 31 (t); John Iacono, 19 (tl), 27 (b), 28, 41 (b), 43 (all), 44 (all), 47 (t),
    58 (b), 60 (b); John W. McDonough, 8 (l), 26 (t), 61; Lane Stewart, 11 (t); Manny Millan, 27 (t), 40; Mark
    Kauffman, 22 (b), 23, 24 (b); Peter Read Miller, 56; Richard Meek, 37; Robert Beck, 20 (b), 24 (t), 29 (b),
    35 (t), 48 (t); Simon Bruty, 55 (t); Walter Iooss Jr., cover (tr), 17 (b), 42, 52 (t)
Wikipedia/Ewen and Donabel, 30

Printed in the United States of America in North Mankato, Minnesota.
122011   006506R

TABLE OF CONTENTS

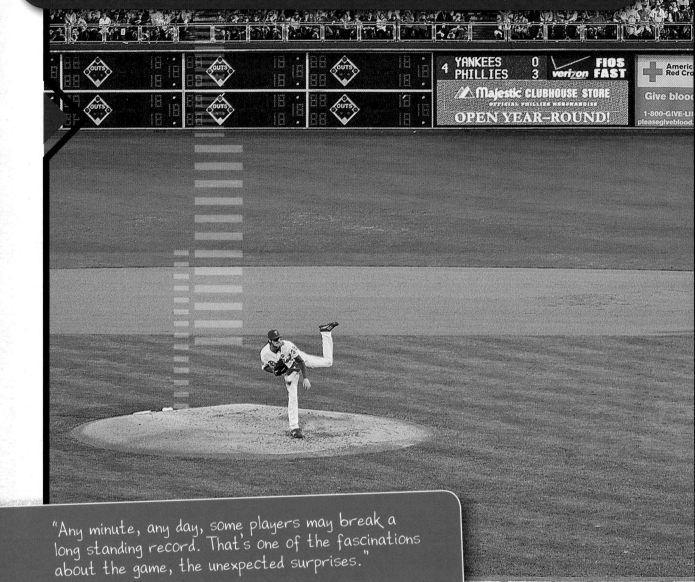

THE BEST OF BASEBALL

4 YANKEES 0 | verizon **FIOS FAST**
PHILLIES 3

Majestic **CLUBHOUSE STORE**
OFFICIAL PHILLIES MERCHANDISE
OPEN YEAR-ROUND!

American Red Cross

Give blood
1-800-GIVE-LIFE
pleasegiveblood.

"Any minute, any day, some players may break a long standing record. That's one of the fascinations about the game, the unexpected surprises."

Connie Mack, manager of the Philadelphia Athletics

Today fans wave wildly on Jumbotrons and umpires use instant replay on home runs, but baseball is similar to the game of old. Americans' interest in baseball dates all the way back to the Civil War era. Back then players fielded with their bare hands, one baseball was used for an entire game, and the bases were made of canvas and filled with sand. Although baseball has made some changes since

the early days, it's still a game of hits, runs, and errors. Sometimes it comes down to one pitch, when clutch players lead their teams to victory. Each year rivalries are relived while teams battle in pursuit of a World Series title. With a rich history, superstar players, and crowd-roaring games, it's easy to see how baseball has long been America's national pastime.

CHAPTER 1

BASEBALL BIOGRAPHY

FAMOUS FIRSTS

Professionals have been playing baseball in organized leagues for more than 100 years. Baseball has a rich history of star players, brilliant coaches, and historic ballparks. But to see how legendary baseball really is, look back to the "firsts" of the game.

The Pittsburgh National League Baseball Club

FIRST BASEBALL REFERENCE

The first record of baseball dates back to 1760. The reference to the sport was found in a woodcut from *A Pretty Little Pocket-Book* in England. The picture is of young boys standing by posts. One of the boys is holding a ball as if about to pitch it. There is even a verse titled "Base-Ball." It reads: "The Ball once struck off / Away flies the Boy / To the next destin'd Post / And then Home with Joy."

FIRST RULES

Alexander Cartwright of the Knickerbocker Base Ball Club of New York helped create the first known list of baseball rules. The rules were known as The Knickerbocker Rules.

FIRST GAME

On June 19, 1846, the first recorded game was played at Elysian Fields in Hoboken, New Jersey. The Knickerbocker Club of New York City took on The New York Club. The New York Club won 23-1.

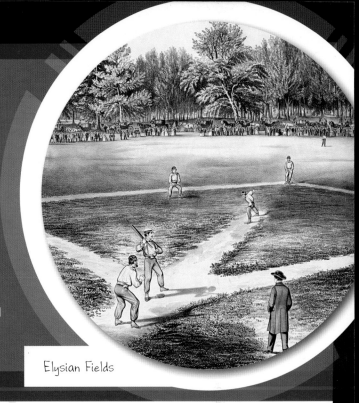

Elysian Fields

FIRST LEAGUES

The National Association of Base Ball Players formed in 1857 and had 22 teams from New York City. The longest-surviving league is the National League. The league started in 1876 with eight teams: The Boston Red Caps, Chicago White Stockings, Cincinnati Red Stockings, Hartford Dark Blues, Louisville Grays, New York Mutuals, Philadelphia Athletics, and St. Louis Brown Stockings. Today the National League has 16 teams. The National League, along with the American League that was formed in 1901, make up Major League Baseball.

FIRST PROFESSIONAL TEAM

In 1869 the Cincinnati Red Stockings paid 10 players to star on its team. Brothers Harry and George Wright were the team's best players. They led the Red Stockings to a record of 57 victories and one tie.

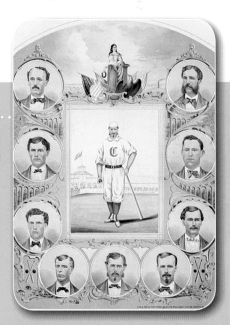

THE FIELD

On a bright, sunny July afternoon, nothing beats cheering for the home baseball team at a fan-packed stadium. From the type of playing surface to the depth of the home run fence, no two baseball stadiums are the same. The game is played both indoors and outdoors, on grass and artificial turf, and in the afternoon or at night.

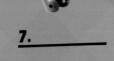

7. _____

FOUL LINE

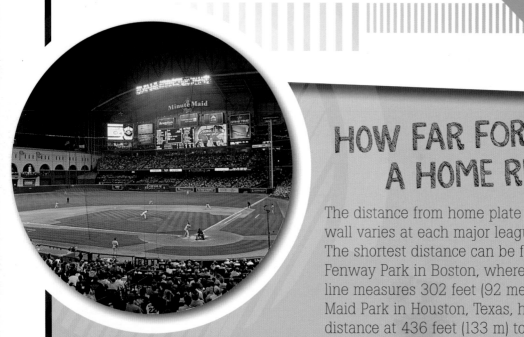

Minute Maid Park

HOW FAR FOR A HOME RUN?

The distance from home plate to the outfield wall varies at each major league ballpark. The shortest distance can be found at Fenway Park in Boston, where the right field line measures 302 feet (92 meters). Minute Maid Park in Houston, Texas, has the longest distance at 436 feet (133 m) to center field.

8. _____

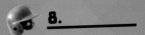

TRIVIA

Name that Position!

Can you match each position with the correct helmet?

PITCHER
CATCHER
FIRST BASEMAN
SECOND BASEMAN
THIRD BASEMAN
SHORTSTOP
LEFTFIELDER
CENTERFIELDER
RIGHTFIELDER

9. _____

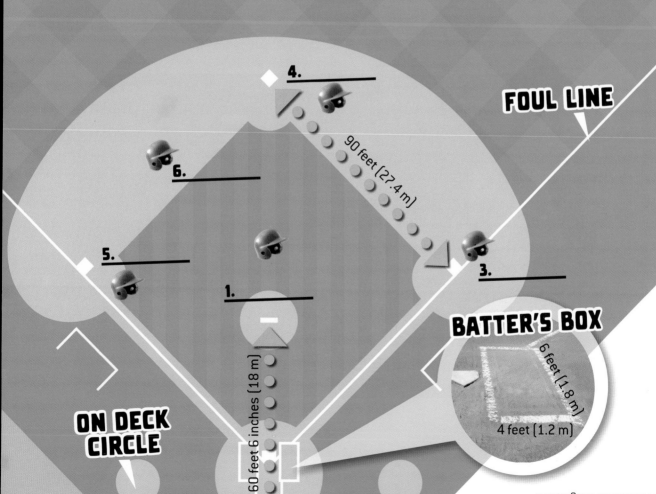

4. _____

FOUL LINE

90 feet (27.4 m)

6. _____

5. _____

3. _____

1. _____

BATTER'S BOX

6 feet (1.8 m)

4 feet (1.2 m)

ON DECK CIRCLE

60 feet 6 inches (18 m)

2. _____

1. Pitcher 2. Catcher 3. First Baseman 4. Second Baseman 5. Third Baseman 6. Shortstop 7. Leftfielder 8. Centerfielder 9. Rightfielder

EQUIPMENT

BATS

Although the origins of the baseball bat vary, one of the most popular bat brands started in 1884. Young Bud Hillerich worked for his father's woodworking company in Louisville, Kentucky. He was watching a local baseball game when Pete "The Old Gladiator" Browning of the Louisville Eclipse broke his bat. After the game Hillerich offered to make Browning a new bat at his father's shop. Hillerich spent all night crafting Browning's new stick, and Browning went 3-for-3 with it the next day. Hillerich kept on making bats, and other major leaguers started asking for them. The bats became so popular that he decided to name them: Louisville Sluggers.

Early baseball bats were much heavier than modern ones. They were made of ash, maple, hickory, or pine. Beginning in the 1970s, aluminum bats gained popularity and were used in Little League and college baseball. But the major leagues have always stuck with wood bats. Many fans prefer to hear the "crack" of wood as opposed to the "ping" of aluminum when bat meets ball.

A Louisville Slugger bat being made from a block of wood

FACT:

In 1905 Honus Wagner, legendary shortstop for the Pittsburgh Pirates, was the first major league ballplayer to endorse a baseball bat. He struck a deal with Bud Hillerich, owner of Hillerich and Bradsby. After the deal was made, the company was allowed to put Wagner's name on its bats.

BALLS

Think of how many baseballs are used during a baseball game. The ball needs to be replaced with every home run and foul ball that reaches the fans. The umpire will even replace the ball if it gets scuffed in the dirt during a pitch. Teams can go through 60 to 70 baseballs in a single game. That can add up to more than 170,000 baseballs during the regular season. It's no wonder these balls are mass-produced.

A baseball has a rubber cork at the core that is wrapped by yarn and covered in stitched leather. The earliest baseballs were all handmade. The balls ended up slightly different from one another. In fact, the baseballs could be "live," "medium," or "dead," depending on what the teams wanted. Live baseballs contained more rubber, while dead ones contained less rubber and occasionally sawdust, yarn, or string. In the 1800s only one or two balls were used per game. By the end of the game, balls were scuffed, dirtied, or even mushy. Albert Spalding, one of baseball's first great pitchers, began making baseballs in Chicago after his playing career. Spalding baseballs were used in the major leagues until 1977, when Rawlings baseballs replaced them as the official baseball.

GLOVES

Players fielded baseballs barehanded until about 1870. As pitchers began to throw with greater speed, the players—especially catchers—started wearing gloves. The first gloves were fingerless and usually made of leather. By 1900 fielding gloves were being used by most players. At the 1904 Louisiana Purchase Exposition, Spalding sporting goods showed off award-winning gloves. Some with webbing between the forefinger and thumb cost from $1.50 to $3. Modern day baseball gloves are designed for each position. The best ones sell for hundreds of dollars.

THE FIRST FIVE

The Baseball Hall of Fame in Cooperstown, New York, is a shrine to the best of baseball. In 1936 five men became the first players in the Hall, which today has about 300 members.

TY COBB

Ty Cobb was one of the most talented—and temperamental—players to ever slide into second base. A competitor in every sense of the word, Cobb retired with a career batting average of .367—the highest in pro baseball history.

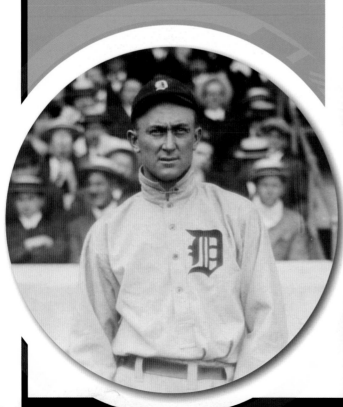

BABE RUTH

George Herman Ruth was bigger than the game in his playing days and remains so today. Known as the Bambino and the Sultan of Swat, the Babe pounded 714 home runs during his career.

CHRISTY MATHEWSON

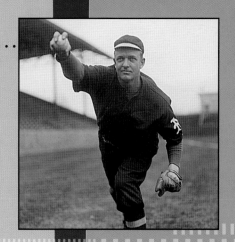

Christy Mathewson employed a hard-to-hit fadeaway pitch called the screwball. The pitch led him to 79 career shutouts and 373 wins. A strict Christian who never pitched on Sundays, Mathewson later served in the U.S. Army during World War I. He was accidentally gassed during a training exercise and developed tuberculosis, which led to his death about six years later at age 45.

WALTER JOHNSON

"The Big Train" was famous for his overpowering fastball delivered in a sidearm motion. He earned 417 wins and 3,509 strikeouts in 21 seasons. Johnson led the Washington Senators to the World Series in 1924 and got the win in the Senators' seventh-game, series-clinching victory. His shutout total of 110 is the most in pro baseball history.

HONUS WAGNER

"The Flying Dutchman" led the National League in batting eight times, slugging six times, and stolen bases five times. His career batting average was .328, even though he swung an unusually heavy bat. Many consider Wagner the greatest shortstop ever to play the game.

CHAPTER 2

TREMENDOUS TEAMS

AROUND THE MAJORS

Thirty teams make up Major League Baseball—14 in the American League and 16 in the National League. Each league has three divisions: East, Central, and West.

The postseason features each of the division winners and a wild card team from each league. The winners from the AL and the NL battle it out in the World Series.

AMERICAN LEAGUE

AL EAST

Baltimore Orioles—Between 1966 and 1983, the Orioles had 18 consecutive winning seasons.

Boston Red Sox—After sending Babe Ruth to the New York Yankees in 1919, the Red Sox endured "The Curse of the Bambino" for 86 years before winning the 2004 World Series.

New York Yankees—With 27 World Series titles, the Yankees have won the most championships in major league history.

Tampa Bay Rays—Rays fans watch their team play at "The Trop" (Tropicana Field), the last nonretractable domed stadium in baseball.

Toronto Blue Jays—The Blue Jays' first game was nearly snowed out in 1977 at Toronto's Exhibition Stadium.

AL CENTRAL

Chicago White Sox—The underdog White Sox bested the favored Cubs in an all-Chicago World Series in 1906.

Cleveland Indians—Cleveland's organization began in 1901 and was formerly nicknamed the Blues, the Bronchos, and the Naps before becoming the Indians in 1915.

Detroit Tigers—In 1984 the Tigers led their division the entire season and ended the year with a World Series win.

Kansas City Royals—The Royals began play in 1969 and fielded a winning team in just their third season.

Minnesota Twins—Before moving to Minnesota, the Twins were the Washington Senators, dating all the way back to 1901.

AL WEST

Los Angeles Angels of Anaheim—An expansion team in 1961, the Angels were already posting a winning record in their second season.

Oakland Athletics—The Athletics were one of the first eight charter teams and were first based in Philadelphia.

Seattle Mariners—In 2001 the Mariners tied the major league record with 116 wins, but they lost in the second round of the playoffs.

Texas Rangers—In 2010 the Rangers reached the World Series for the first time in franchise history.

NATIONAL LEAGUE

NL CENTRAL

Chicago Cubs—The Cubs have the longest streak without a World Series championship at 103 years.

Cincinnati Reds—The Reds take their name from the oldest club in pro baseball history, the Cincinnati Red Stockings of 1869.

Houston Astros—The Astros played in the Astrodome, baseball's first domed stadium, before moving in 2000 into Minute Maid Park, an outdoor ballpark with a retractable roof.

Milwaukee Brewers—In 2007 first baseman Prince Fielder became the first Brewer and the youngest player to hit 50 home runs in a single season.

Pittsburgh Pirates—The Pirates were a force in the early days of the National League and met Boston in 1903 for the first World Series.

St. Louis Cardinals—The Cardinals have won 10 World Series titles, second only to the Yankees.

NL EAST

Atlanta Braves—The Braves won the NL East an impressive 11 straight times from 1995 to 2005.

Florida Marlins—The Marlins have never won the NL East Division, but they have won the World Series twice—in 1997 and 2003.

New York Mets—The "Amazin' Mets" of 1969 won 39 of their final 50 regular season games and clubbed the Baltimore Orioles 4-1 to win their first World Series.

Philadelphia Phillies—The Phillies changed their name to the Philadelphia Blue Jays for the 1943 and 1944 seasons only.

Washington Nationals—Before the team was purchased in 2006, the Nationals spent a few years as the only league-owned team in Major League Baseball.

NL WEST

Arizona Diamondbacks—The Diamondbacks were around for only four years before winning their first World Series title in 2001.

Colorado Rockies—The Rockies play in Major League Baseball's most home run-friendly stadium, Coors Field.

Los Angeles Dodgers—The Dodgers moved to the West Coast in 1958 after spending their first 74 years in Brooklyn.

San Diego Padres—The Padres won NL pennants in 1984 and 1998, but they lost in the World Series both times.

San Francisco Giants—The Giants won the 2010 World Series, their first championship since 1954.

Name the eight MLB teams with animal nicknames.

Answer: Blue Jays, Cardinals, Cubs, Diamondbacks, Marlins, Orioles, Rays, Tigers

WORLD SERIES GREATS

1907 CHICAGO CUBS

Though the 1906 Cubs won a major league record 116 games—a record that only the 2001 Seattle Mariners have tied—they dropped the World Series to the Chicago White Sox. The Cubs made up for it in 1907, going 107–45 and taking the World Series from the Detroit Tigers. Leading the way for the 1907 Cubs was the talented double-play combination of shortstop Joe Tinker, second baseman Johnny Evers, and first baseman Frank Chance. They also had a fine pitching staff of Orval Overall (23–7), Mordecai "Three Finger" Brown (20–6), Carl Lundgren (18–7), and "Big" Ed Reulbach (17–4). The Cubs also won the 1908 World Series.

The second West Side Park, home of the Chicago Cubs, 1893–1915

1927 NEW YORK YANKEES

After losing the 1926 World Series to the St. Louis Cardinals four games to three, the '27 Yankees were hungry for victory. Their "Murderer's Row" lineup featured Babe Ruth (60 HR) and Lou Gehrig (.373 BA, 47 HR, 175 RBIs). Three others batted better than .300: centerfielder Earle Combs, leftfielder Bob Meusel, and second baseman Tony Lazzeri. The Yankees finished 110–44 and swept the World Series from the Pittsburgh Pirates in four games.

1961 NEW YORK YANKEES

Mickey Mantle and Roger Maris spent much of the 1961 season on a home run tear. They were both trying to break Babe Ruth's legendary record of 60 home runs in a season. Fan-favorite Mantle came close with 54 by season's end. But Maris was the one to surpass Ruth by belting 61 homers. First baseman Moose Skowron contributed 28 homers, and catcher-turned-leftfielder Yogi Berra bashed 22. Whitey Ford led the Yankees' pitching staff (and the American League) with a 25–4 record. Reliever Luis Arroyo was impressive out of the bullpen with a 15–5 record and 29 saves. The 1961 Yankees finished 109–53 and beat the Cincinnati Reds four games to one in the World Series.

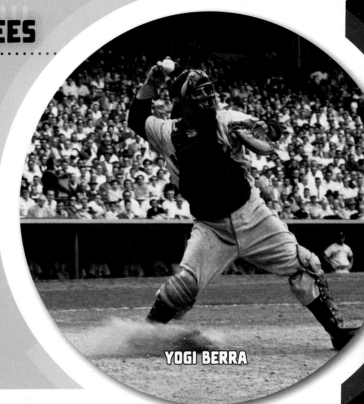

YOGI BERRA

1975 CINCINNATI REDS

Cincinnati's "Big Red Machine" was the pride of Major League Baseball in the mid-1970s. Managed by the colorful Sparky Anderson, the 1975 Reds went 108–54. They featured third baseman Pete Rose, shortstop Dave Concepcion, second baseman Joe Morgan, and first baseman Tony Perez. They also had two outfielders—George Foster and Ken Griffey Sr.—who hit .300 that season. Talented catcher Johnny Bench handled a solid pitching staff. The Reds' seven-game World Series victory over the Red Sox was one of baseball's most exciting ever. Cincinnati repeated as champions in 1976.

Catcher Johnny Bench celebrates with pitcher Will McEnaney after winning the 1975 World Series.

TURN OF THE 21ST CENTURY TEAM

There is no shortage of superstars in the MLB today. These power sluggers, pitching aces, and gold glove fielders are regulars at the annual All-Star Game.

CATCHER

Joe Mauer of the Minnesota Twins became the first catcher to win an American League batting title in 2006. That year, at the age of 23, he hit for a .347 average. He added two more batting titles in 2008 and 2009 and has a cannon for a throwing arm. Ivan "Pudge" Rodriguez has caught more games than any other backstop in major league history.

JOE MAUER

STARTING PITCHERS

In 2001 Roger Clemens and Randy Johnson paired to win the NL and AL Cy Young Awards. Clemens won a record seven Cy Youngs, and Johnson took home five of his own. Each had overpowering fastballs and intimidating demeanors. Righty Tim Lincecum is an up-and-comer for the San Francisco Giants who won back-to-back Cy Youngs in 2008 and 2009.

MARIANO RIVERA

RELIEF PITCHERS

Mariano Rivera was the backbone of the bullpen for five New York Yankees World Series championship teams. He has saved more ballgames than any closer in American League history. Trevor Hoffman of the San Diego Padres and Milwaukee Brewers is the all-time MLB saves leader with 601.

FIRST BASE

St. Louis Cardinals slugger Albert Pujols is a home run-smashing, high average-hitting, defensive force of nature at first base. He already has MVPs in 2005, 2008, and 2009 to show for it. Ryan Howard of the Philadelphia Phillies and Justin Morneau of the Minnesota Twins are also homer-slamming beasts who have each won MVPs.

ALBERT PUJOLS

SECOND BASE

Roberto Alomar was a great all-around second baseman who played 17 seasons for a variety of teams. Dustin Pedroia of the Boston Red Sox captured AL Rookie of the Year in 2007 and MVP in 2008. The Philadelphia Phillies' Chase Utley combines power with speed and can hit for average.

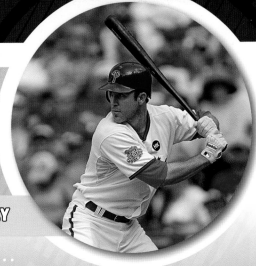

CHASE UTLEY

THIRD BASE

Chipper Jones of the Braves has had a successful career and has continued to play through injuries. Michael Young of the Texas Rangers and David Wright of the New York Mets can play the hot corner with the best of them. Talented Evan Longoria of the Tampa Bay Rays is certain to be a continued smash in future years.

DAVID WRIGHT

SHORTSTOP

Derek Jeter of the Yankees is the standard to which all modern day shortstops compare themselves. The high-average hitter has a way of making hard plays look easy and clutch plays look routine. Marlins' shortstop Hanley Ramirez uses his speed on the base paths but can also hit the long ball.

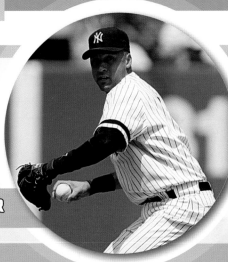

DEREK JETER

OUTFIELD

One of the purest hitters in the major leagues is Ichiro Suzuki of the Seattle Mariners. The fleet-footed outfielder won both the AL Rookie of the Year and MVP awards in 2001. Ken Griffey Jr. unleashed his signature left-handed swing for more than 20 seasons. The Brewers' Ryan Braun, Dodgers' Matt Kemp, and Rangers' Josh Hamilton are all on their way to stardom.

JOSH HAMILTON

WORLDLY COMPETITION

In 2006 the first World Baseball Classic was played with approval by the International Baseball Federation. The event is a tournament of 16 teams from around the world. The first tournament was held in March, before the start of the 2006 Major League Baseball season. Many American fans and players were skeptical of the tournament at first. They blamed the WBC for the failure of baseball as an Olympic sport. They also claimed that many American players were not interested in the tournament. But as the WBC drew near, the U.S. had convinced some of its best players to compete, including infielders Derek Jeter and Alex Rodriguez, outfielder Ken Griffey Jr., and pitchers Roger Clemens and Joe Nathan.

Derrek Lee celebrates after hitting a home run against Mexico in 2006.

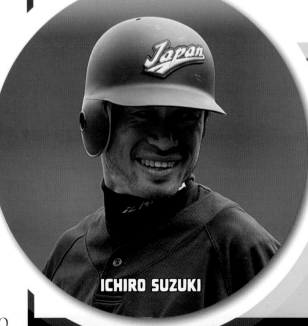

ICHIRO SUZUKI

The WBC's 16 teams were Australia, Canada, China, Chinese Taipei, Cuba, Dominican Republic, Italy, Japan, Mexico, Netherlands, Panama, Puerto Rico, South Africa, South Korea, United States, and Venezuela. South Korea fared extremely well by winning all six of its pool games, but it turned out that Japan had the best team. Japan featured outfielder Ichiro Suzuki, who starred in Japan for nearly nine seasons before joining the Seattle Mariners in 2001. Japan defeated Cuba 10-6 to win the 2006 WBC title.

The WBC turned out to be wildly successful. Many countries had convinced their best players—many of them U.S. major leaguers—to play in the event. Fans' national loyalties ran high enough that another WBC was played in 2009. Japan again trumped the field, downing the United States in the semifinals and South Korea in the championship. Plans have been made to hold the next WBC in 2013.

Cuba won a round-one game against the Netherlands.

OLYMPIC BASEBALL

Though baseball was played as an Olympic medal sport from 1992 to 2008, it is not included in the 2012 Olympics. A main problem is that the Summer Olympics are played every four years during the heart of the Major League Baseball season. This left many of the sport's best players unavailable for Olympic play.

American minor-leaguer Bobby Kingsbury played for Greece during the 2004 Olympics.

NEGRO LEAGUES DREAM TEAM

Until Jackie Robinson broke the color barrier in 1947, African-Americans were not allowed to play in Major League Baseball. But under the guidance of black owner/manager Rube Foster, the Negro National League was born in 1920 and the Eastern Colored League three years later. Then the Negro American League was born in 1937. These leagues boasted some of the greatest baseball players from around the nation. Each position featured its share of superstars.

Brown Jackson after hitting a home run during the 1958 Negro Leagues' All-Star Game

PITCHER

Leroy "Satchel" Paige was probably the most well known of all Negro Leagues players. When not skipping from team to team, Paige led his own baseball squad on cross-country trips. As a 42-year-old major league rookie, he signed with the Cleveland Indians during the 1948 season and helped them to the World Series. (Paige's age has always been in question, and some baseball experts believe he was more than 50 years old when he made it to the big leagues.) Paige pitched parts of six seasons in the majors.

CATCHER

The powerful Josh Gibson led the Negro Leagues in homers for 10 straight years, hitting a reported 75 in 1931. Roy Campanella started playing in the Negro Leagues at age 15. He spent nine years in the league before moving on to a successful major league career with the Dodgers.

ROY CAMPANELLA

FIRST BASE

Walter "Buck" Leonard was a talented left-handed power hitter. He paired with Josh Gibson to lead Pittsburgh's Homestead Grays to nine consecutive Negro Leagues championships between 1937 and 1945. The even-keeled Leonard was also a tough defender who made difficult fielding plays look simple.

SECOND BASE

Martin Dihigo was born in Cuba and started his career playing for the Cuban Stars in 1923. He later played for the Hilldale Daisies, Baltimore Black Sox, and New York Cubans. He often played second base but also played every other position, including pitcher.

SHORTSTOP

Jackie Robinson played one season at shortstop and batted .345 with the Kansas City Monarchs in 1945. In 1947 he famously broke Major League Baseball's color barrier by suiting up with the Brooklyn Dodgers. Another great shortstop, John Henry "Pop" Lloyd, was a defensive pro. He dug out grounders so smoothly that he was nicknamed "The Tablespoon." Even the great Babe Ruth once referred to Lloyd as the best ballplayer of all time.

Jackie Robinson, 1955 World Series

THIRD BASE

William Julius "Judy" Johnson starred for most of his Negro Leagues career with the Hilldale Daisies. He had a hard-hitting right-handed stroke at the plate. In the field he had a sure glove and strong arm at the hot corner.

OUTFIELD

James "Cool Papa" Bell was so fast that people claimed he could flick the light switch off in his bedroom and be in bed before the room got dark. George "Mule" Suttles and Norman "Turkey" Stearns were cream-of-the-crop long-ball hitters. Oscar Charleston was compared to major league greats Babe Ruth and Ty Cobb.

FACT:

Hank Aaron was the last player from the Negro Leagues to make the major leagues. His Negro Leagues experience lasted less than one season. Aaron batted .467 as an 18-year-old rookie with the Indianapolis Clowns, which won the Negro American League title in 1952. From there Aaron went on to an incredible 23-season career in Major League Baseball. He retired in 1976 with 755 home runs.

CHAPTER 3

PRIME-TIME PLAYERS

ALL-TIME SLUGGERS

On August 7, 2007, Barry Bonds hit his record-breaking 756th career home run.

Home Runs

1.	Barry Bonds	762
2.	Hank Aaron	755
3.	Babe Ruth	714
4.	Willie Mays	660
5.	Ken Griffey Jr.	630
6.	Alex Rodriguez*	613
7.	Sammy Sosa	609
8.	Jim Thome*	589
9.	Frank Robinson	586
10.	Mark McGwire	583

RBIs

1.	Hank Aaron	2,297
2.	Babe Ruth	2,213
3.	Cap Anson	2,075
4.	Barry Bonds	1,996
5.	Lou Gehrig	1,995
6.	Stan Musial	1,951
7.	Ty Cobb	1,938
8.	Jimmie Foxx	1,922
9.	Eddie Murray	1,917
10.	Willie Mays	1,903

Stan Musial had 12 walk-off home runs during his career.

Runs

	Player	Runs
1.	Rickey Henderson	2,295
2.	Ty Cobb	2,246
3.	Barry Bonds	2,227
4.	Hank Aaron	2,174
	Babe Ruth	2,174
6.	Pete Rose	2,165
7.	Willie Mays	2,062
8.	Cap Anson	1,999
9.	Stan Musial	1,949
10.	Lou Gehrig	1,888

Willie Mays is one of 15 players who have hit four home runs in one game.

In 1941 Ted Williams became the last player to bat over .400 for an entire season. He batted .407 in 1953 but only had 91 at bats that year.

Batting Average

1.	Ty Cobb	.366
2.	Rogers Hornsby	.359
3.	Joe Jackson	.356
4.	Lefty O'Doul	.349
5.	Ed Delahanty	.346
6.	Tris Speaker	.345
7.	Billy Hamilton	.344
	Ted Williams	.344
9.	Dan Brouthers	.342
	Babe Ruth	.342

*Active players

All statistics are through the 2010 regular season.

FACT:

Babe Ruth is the only player to appear in the career top 10 for home runs, RBIs, runs, and batting average. He averaged better than one home run every 12 at bats for his entire career. The Great Bambino also appears in the top 10 for walks and total bases.

GLOVES OF GOLD

OUTFIELD

Willie Mays is well known for his over-the-shoulder grab in Game 1 of the 1954 World Series. He won 12 Gold Gloves and swung a powerful bat as well. Roberto Clemente was awarded 12 Gold Gloves and selected to 12 All-Star games. Outfielders Ken Griffey Jr. and Torii Hunter have made stealing home runs look easy. And although he played before the Gold Glove existed, speedster Ty Cobb was dynamite in the outfield as well.

TORII HUNTER

PITCHER

When it comes to fielding off the mound, it's hard to argue with Greg Maddux's 18 Gold Gloves, including 13 straight from 1990 to 2002. Jim Kaat won all 16 of his Gold Gloves in a row from 1962 to 1977 while playing for the Twins, White Sox, and Phillies.

CATCHER

Yankees backstop Yogi Berra was one of the most nimble fielders to play his position. He is one of only 11 catchers to ever have a 1.000 fielding percentage for an entire season. Ivan "Pudge" Rodriguez combined great fielding skills with an amazing throwing arm in the 1990s and 2000s.

IVAN RODRIGUEZ

FIRST BASE

George "Boomer" Scott wasn't always solid in the batter's box, but he was always sure-handed in the field. He even nicknamed his beloved glove "Black Beauty." Keith Hernandez of the Mets and Don Mattingly of the Yankees also played a great defense at first base.

SECOND BASE

Whether playing in Philadelphia or Cleveland, Napoleon LaJoie had glue in his glove and could hit with the best. Roberto Alomar earned 10 Gold Gloves in 11 years at second base between 1991 and 2001.

SHORTSTOP

Honus Wagner of the Pirates was hot at both the plate and the infield's toughest position. Light-hitting Ozzie Smith of the Cardinals was nicknamed "The Wizard of Oz" for his acrobatic plays at short.

OZZIE SMITH

THIRD BASE

Brooks Robinson was awarded 16 Gold Gloves from 1960 to 1975. Nicknamed "The Vacuum Cleaner," Robinson also gunned down many baserunners hoping to leg out an infield hit. Mike Schmidt of the Phillies had a solid mitt that won him 10 Gold Gloves.

MIKE SCHMIDT

FACT:

The only brothers to win Gold Gloves were third basemen Ken and Clete Boyer and catchers Bengie and Yadier Molina.

PITCHING ELITE

STRIKEOUT KINGS

Nolan Ryan's strikeout record is one that may never be broken. The ace pitched for 27 seasons, sometimes putting in more than 300 innings in one season. His command on the mound led him to an MLB record seven no-hitters, three more than the previous leader, Sandy Koufax. "The Ryan Express" led the majors in strikeouts seven times.

	Player	Strikeouts
1.	Nolan Ryan	5,714
2.	Randy Johnson	4,875
3.	Roger Clemens	4,672
4.	Steve Carlton	4,136
5.	Bert Blyleven	3,701
6.	Tom Seaver	3,640
7.	Don Sutton	3,574
8.	Gaylord Perry	3,534
9.	Walter Johnson	3,509
10.	Greg Maddux	3,371

NOLAN RYAN

FACT:

Through 2010 the active pitcher with the most strikeouts was 47-year-old Jamie Moyer with 2,405. The youngest active pitcher in the top 100 was 29-year-old CC Sabathia with 1,787.

WINS LEADERS

Pitchers used to start every third or fourth game and pitched all nine innings. Late in the 20th century, managers switched to five-man rotations, and pitchers had fewer chances to rack up wins.

Only 24 pitchers have recorded 300 career wins in MLB history.

	Player	Wins
1.	Cy Young	511
2.	Walter Johnson	417
3.	Pete Alexander	373
4.	Christy Mathewson	373
5.	Pud Galvin	365
6.	Warren Spahn	363
7.	Kid Nichols	361
8.	Greg Maddux	355
9.	Roger Clemens	354
10.	Tim Keefe	342

CY YOUNG

WHAT A RELIEF!

In baseball's earliest days, pitchers who started a game were expected to finish it. It didn't take long to see what happened to the starting pitchers' arms. By the 1960s good bullpens were essential to winning ballclubs.

	Player	Saves
1.	Trevor Hoffman*	601
2.	Mariano Rivera*	559
3.	Lee Smith	478
4.	John Franco	424
5.	Billy Wagner*	422
6.	Dennis Eckersley	390
7.	Jeff Reardon	367
8.	Troy Percival	358
9.	Randy Myers	347
10.	Rollie Fingers	341

TREVOR HOFFMAN

*Active players

All statistics are through the 2010 regular season.

SUPER CY

In 1956 Baseball Commissioner Ford Frick created an award that was given to the best pitcher in the major leagues. It was named after Cy Young, the winner of 511 games—most in the major leagues. Starting in 1967 two Cy Young Awards were given each year, one to the best pitcher in the American League and one in the National League.

Sandy Koufax's 1963 Cy Young Award

SANDY KOUFAX

Sandy Koufax of the Los Angeles Dodgers was the Cy Young winner in 1963. He was the first pitcher to be unanimously voted for the award by the Baseball Writers Association of America. That season the crafty lefthander went 25–5 with a 1.88 ERA and helped the Dodgers to a World Series title. In 1965 and 1966, Koufax added two more Cy Youngs before retiring from baseball at the age of 30.

DWIGHT GOODEN

Dwight Gooden was the youngest pitcher to win the Cy Young at age 20. During his standout 1985 season with the New York Mets, "Doc" went 24–4 with a 1.53 ERA and eight shutouts. He also tallied an amazing 268 strikeouts, best in the National League. The previous season, Gooden's rookie year, he struck out 276 batters with his flaming fastball.

GREG MADDUX & RANDY JOHNSON

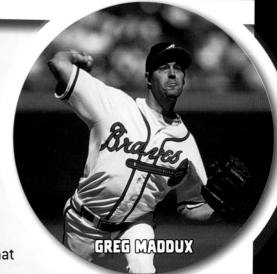

GREG MADDUX

Greg Maddux and Randy Johnson share the record for most seasons in a row (four) of winning the Cy Young Award. Maddux kept a low ERA thanks to his pinpoint control and calm demeanor. On the other hand, Johnson was a fiery competitor. He slung 100-mile-per-hour fastballs that had hitters shaking in their cleats.

YEAR OF THE PITCHER

When it came to baseball in 1968, there was no doubt it was the Year of the Pitcher. Jim "Catfish" Hunter of the Oakland Athletics threw a perfect game against the Minnesota Twins. Tom Phoebus of the Baltimore Orioles, Gaylord Perry of the San Francisco Giants, Ray Washburn of the St. Louis Cardinals, and George Culver of the Cincinnati Reds all threw no-hitters. Luis Tiant of the Cleveland Indians went 21–9 with an American League-best 1.60 ERA. Juan Marichal went 26–9 with an amazing 30 complete games. Don Drysdale of the Los Angeles Dodgers threw eight complete game shutouts that season as well.

JIM "CATFISH" HUNTER

The two pitching standouts of 1968 were Bob Gibson of the St. Louis Cardinals and Denny McLain of the Detroit Tigers. Gibson allowed just 1.12 runs per nine innings and led the majors with 268 strikeouts. He also racked up a 22–9 record that included 13 shutouts. At one point he put together a 95-inning stretch in which he allowed just two runs. McLain won a league-best 31 games with just six losses. He threw 28 complete games—six of which were shutouts—and recorded a 1.96 ERA.

BOB GIBSON

It was a dream matchup when Bob Gibson and Denny McLain faced off in Game 1 of the 1968 World Series. Gibson was nearly unhittable, striking out 17 batters as the Cardinals won 4-0. In Game 4 the pitchers faced off again with Gibson again besting McLain in a 10-1 Cardinals rout. But McLain's teammate Mickey Lolich, a left-handed pitcher who had gone 17–9 in the regular season, won Game 2 and Game 5 for the Tigers in complete-game efforts. McLain pitched a gem to help the Tigers win Game 6. Gibson pitched again in Game 7, but this time, he was topped by Lolich in a tight 4-1 victory.

MICKEY LOLICH

FACT:

After the 1968 season, Major League Baseball lowered the mound from 15 inches to 10 inches and shrunk the strike zone to make it more fair for batters.

MASTERFUL MANAGERS

BOBBY COX

Atlanta Braves, Toronto Blue Jays

Bobby Cox has been ejected more times than any other manager in MLB history. In 2007 he was ejected for the 132nd time, breaking the previous record held by John McGraw. Cox won his lone World Series with the Braves in 1995. He retired after the 2010 season.

TONY LA RUSSA

Chicago White Sox, Oakland Athletics, St. Louis Cardinals

Tony La Russa became the second manager to win World Series rings in both the American League and the National League. (Sparky Anderson was the first.) As of 2010 La Russa has the most career wins among present-day managers with 2,638.

SPARKY ANDERSON

Cincinnati Reds, Detroit Tigers

Sparky Anderson spent only one season in the major leagues as a player. He was a light-hitting second baseman for the Philadelphia Phillies in 1959. But once he turned to managing, he found his true calling. He became the first manager to win World Series titles in both the National League and the American League.

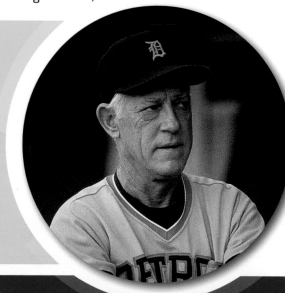

CONNIE MACK

Pittsburgh Pirates, Philadelphia Athletics

One of the earliest managers in the game also played 11 seasons in the late 1800s. Over more than 50 years, Connie Mack racked up a major league record 3,731 regular season wins and five World Series titles.

JOE TORRE
New York Mets, Atlanta Braves, St. Louis Cardinals, New York Yankees, Los Angeles Dodgers

Joe Torre won the National League MVP in 1971 as a catcher and third baseman for the Cardinals. He had a rough start when he switched to managing in 1977, and his Mets didn't have a winning record for five straight seasons. He had good seasons with the Braves and Cardinals before he became successful as the Yankees' manager. He broke a Yankees record with 12 straight playoff appearances with New York, before heading to L.A. . . . .

JOE MCCARTHY
Chicago Cubs, New York Yankees, Boston Red Sox

In 24 seasons Joe McCarthy set the record for best winning percentage with a 2,125–1,333 record. He won seven World Series titles, all with the Yankees.

CASEY STENGEL
Brooklyn Dodgers, Boston Bees/Braves, New York Yankees, New York Mets

"The Old Perfessor" won a record five straight World Series titles with the Yankees from 1949 to 1953. Casey Stengel won two more titles in 1956 and 1958. He holds the record for most World Series games won with 37.

JOHN MCGRAW
Baltimore Orioles, New York Giants

"Little Napoleon" was tough on his players, but he was also a successful manager. John McGraw captured the most pennants in major league history with 10 for the Giants. He also served as a player during eight of his managing seasons.

42 FOREVER

In 1997 Major League Baseball retired the number 42 for all its teams. The man who wore number 42 was Jackie Robinson. Fifty years earlier he became the first player to break the color barrier in Major League Baseball.

Jackie Robinson's 42 hangs at each stadium next to the other retired numbers of the home team's players.

TRIVIA

Match the player to the retired number and team.

Craig Biggio	24, Athletics
Dave Concepcion	21, Braves
Bob Feller	7, Astros
Carlton Fisk	41 , Mets
Rickey Henderson	19, Indians
Roger Maris	13, Reds
Ryne Sandberg	72, White Sox
Tom Seaver	1, Cardinals
Ozzie Smith	9, Yankees
Warren Spahn	23, Cubs

Answer: Biggio—7; Concepcion—13; Feller—19; Fisk—72; Henderson—24; Maris—9; Sandberg—23; Seaver—41; Smith—1; Spahn—21

Jackie Robinson was born in 1919 and grew up in California as the youngest of five children. He showed promise in athletics from an early age. In high school he excelled in track and field, basketball, football, tennis, and baseball. He continued his athletic career in college but left just before graduation.

In 1942 Robinson entered the military. He was honorably discharged after a racial incident and began looking for employment. Though he was an incredibly gifted athlete, none of the sports he loved to play employed African-Americans in the major leagues.

Robinson tried his hand as a coach and athletic director at a university, a professional football player in a minor league, and a shortstop for the Kansas City Monarchs of the Negro Baseball Leagues. Then Branch Rickey, president of the Brooklyn Dodgers, signed him to a minor league contract in 1945. Robinson worked his way up from there.

On April 15, 1947, Robinson started as a 28-year-old first baseman for the Dodgers in a game at Ebbets Field. He finished the season with a .297 batting average, 12 home runs, and a league-leading 29 stolen bases—good enough for Rookie of the Year honors. Robinson played for 10 seasons with the Dodgers, hitting a .311 lifetime batting average and making six All-Star squads.

FACT:

Lou Gehrig of the New York Yankees was the first player in the major leagues—and any sport—whose number was retired. Gehrig's number 4 was retired by New York in 1939 after his retirement from baseball. He had a condition called amyotrophic lateral sclerosis (ALS), now known as Lou Gehrig's disease. Gehrig died from it in 1941 at the age of 37.

CHAPTER 4

REMARKABLE RECORDS

FANTASTIC 56

Joe DiMaggio makes the last put out in the 1941 World Series.

On May 15, 1941, New York Yankees outfielder Joe DiMaggio took his bat to the plate and hit a single off Chicago White Sox pitcher Eddie Smith. Little did anyone know that DiMaggio had just started a record streak. A full two months—and 56 games—would pass before DiMaggio failed to get at least one hit in a game. To this day DiMaggio's record 56-game hitting streak has never been topped. In fact, only Pete Rose (44-game streak in 1978) and Paul Molitor (39-game streak in 1987) have come close.

During the 56 games, DiMaggio collected 91 hits in 223 at bats for a .409 batting average. Of those 91 hits, 56 were singles, 16 were doubles, four were triples, and 15 were home runs. The streak ended at the hands of the Cleveland Indians on July 17. Indians third baseman Ken Keltner twice robbed DiMaggio of hits with outstanding defensive plays.

DiMaggio's streak kick-started a sluggish Yankees team. New York went on to win the 1941 World Series over the Brooklyn Dodgers. DiMaggio finished the year with a .357 batting average, 30 homers, and 125 RBIs. He won the AL Most Valuable Player award over Boston Red Sox leftfielder Ted Williams, who batted an amazing .406 for the entire season.

61 IN '61

New York Yankees slugger Babe Ruth was the game's first true power hitter. He was also the first player to smash more than 50 home runs in a single season when he hit 54 in 1920. He upped that record to 59 homers in 1921. He then hit 60 in 1927—a mark that would stand for 34 years. Ruth finished his career with 714 home runs, another mark that would stand for 39 years.

Hack Wilson (56 HRs in 1930), Jimmie Foxx (58 HRs in 1932), and Hank Greenberg (58 HRs in 1938), challenged Ruth's single-season home run record but fell short. Finally, outfielder Roger Maris of the Yankees bested Ruth's record by bashing 61 home runs in 1961. Sadly for Maris, because of Ruth's fame, he was often booed—and even threatened—during his pursuit of the record. To make matters worse for Maris, many people argued that his 61 homers should go into the record books with an asterisk next to it. They stated that Maris had more games during the season to hit 61 home runs than Ruth had to hit his 60 home runs.

"They acted as though I was doing something wrong, poisoning the record books or something," said Maris years later. "Do you know what I have to show for sixty-one home runs? Nothing. Exactly nothing."

BABE RUTH

IRON MAN STREAK

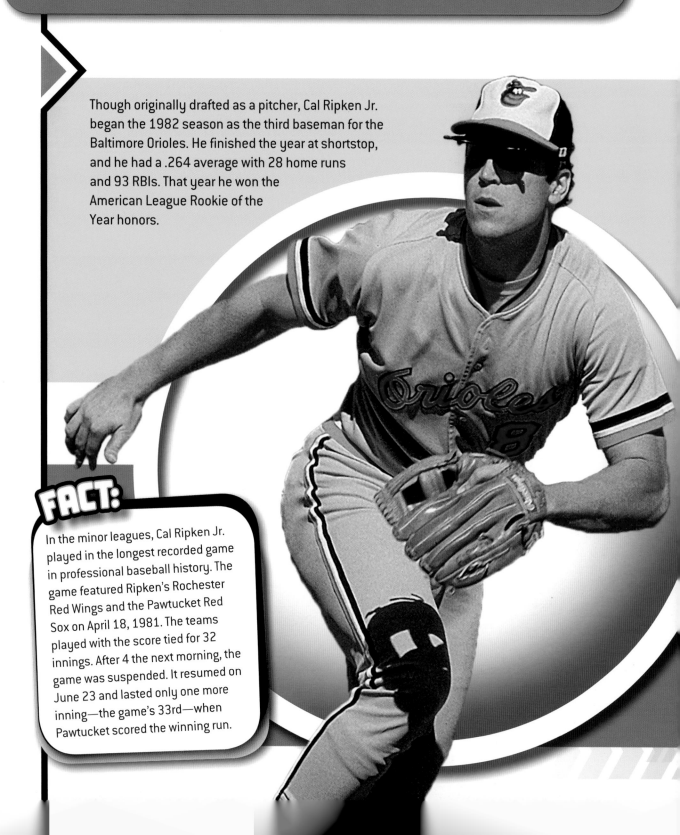

Though originally drafted as a pitcher, Cal Ripken Jr. began the 1982 season as the third baseman for the Baltimore Orioles. He finished the year at shortstop, and he had a .264 average with 28 home runs and 93 RBIs. That year he won the American League Rookie of the Year honors.

FACT:

In the minor leagues, Cal Ripken Jr. played in the longest recorded game in professional baseball history. The game featured Ripken's Rochester Red Wings and the Pawtucket Red Sox on April 18, 1981. The teams played with the score tied for 32 innings. After 4 the next morning, the game was suspended. It resumed on June 23 and lasted only one more inning—the game's 33rd—when Pawtucket scored the winning run.

In 1983 the Orioles had a remarkable season and won the World Series. Ripken became a true fixture in the lineup, playing all 162 games and batting .318 with 27 homers and 102 RBIs. He also made his very first All-Star team and went on to win the AL Most Valuable Player award. In 1987 Ripken's father Cal Sr., a longtime Orioles minor league coach, was promoted to manager of the major league club. He managed not only his son Cal Jr., but his son Billy, an Orioles second baseman. The Orioles fell on hard times in 1988, starting the season with a major league record 21 losses. Though Ripken Sr. was fired as manager during the team's losing streak, the junior Ripken kept playing his usual steady game, coming to the ballpark every day to work and play hard.

By the 1995 season, Ripken hadn't missed a game since May 30, 1982. He was closing in on New York Yankees first baseman Lou Gehrig's record of 2,130 games played in a row. Most people thought Gehrig's record was unbreakable.

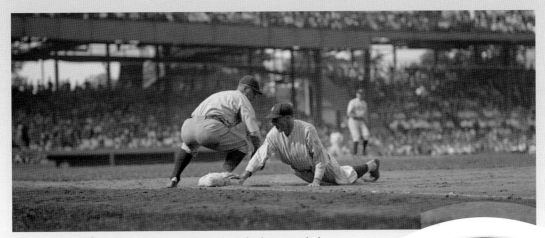

Lou Gehrig slides safely back to first base.

On September 6, 1995, Ripken stepped onto the field for the 2,131st consecutive game. President Bill Clinton was in attendance and watched as Ripken thrilled his home fans by cranking a home run in the fourth inning. After the visitors' half of the fifth inning, when the game was in the books, Ripken had officially beaten the record. He made a loop around the field to high-five fans in celebration as he was given a standing ovation that lasted more than 20 minutes. Ripken's streak lasted until September 20, 1998, when it ended at 2,632 games.

Cal Ripken's fourth-inning home run trot, September 6, 1995

41

CLUTCH HOMERS OF OCTOBER

OCTOBER 3, 1951

Capping an amazing, end-of-the-season comeback, the New York Giants downed the Brooklyn Dodgers at New York's Polo Grounds to win the pennant. In the third game of a three-game playoff, with the Giants down by two runs, Giants outfielder Bobby Thomson belted a three-run homer in the bottom of the ninth inning. The Giants won the game 5-4. The homer was nicknamed the "shot heard round the world."

OCTOBER 3, 1960

The 1960 World Series pitted the hard-hitting New York Yankees against the Pittsburgh Pirates. The teams split the first six games, but New York had dominated the field. The Yankees won by 10 or more runs, while the Pirates' biggest victory was by three runs. In Game 7 the Pirates mounted a 5-run, eighth inning rally to take the lead, but the Yankees tied the game in the top of the ninth. In the bottom of the inning, the first Pirates batter, Bill Mazeroski, smashed a 1-0 pitch over the left field wall, giving the underdog Pirates the World Series crown. Mazeroski entered the record books with the first walk-off home run to win a World Series.

OCTOBER 21, 1975

In 1975 the Cincinnati Reds and Boston Red Sox met in an epic World Series battle. Red Sox catcher Carlton Fisk hit a shot down the left field line. The ball was definitely going to clear the fence, but it looked like it might go foul. Fisk waved his arms as he ran down the first base line, begging the ball to stay fair. The ball cleared the fence in fair territory, and the Red Sox won the game. Despite Fisk's heroics, the Reds took the series with a 4-3 win in Game 7.

OCTOBER 15, 1988

The Dodgers' star outfielder Kirk Gibson had been hampered by a bad hamstring. Most people thought he was unavailable to play in the World Series. But the crowd went wild as Gibson limped to the plate as a pinch-hitter in the ninth inning of Game 1 versus the Oakland A's. He smashed the game-winning home run into the right field stands. Though it was Gibson's only plate appearance of the series, it set the tone for a Dodgers championship.

OCTOBER 26, 1991

The Atlanta Braves led the 1991 World Series three games to two. Game 6 went into extra innings, and fans were at the edge of their seats with every out. In the bottom of the 11th inning, centerfielder Kirby Puckett of the Minnesota Twins sent the home fans into a frenzy by walloping a home run to win the game. Earlier in the game, Puckett had also made an amazing high-flying grab at the outfield fence to save a run. The Twins won Game 7, 1-0, to take home the World Series title.

OCTOBER 23, 1993

During the 1993 World Series, Toronto led the series 3–2. In Game 6 the Philadelphia Phillies were up 6-5 in the ninth inning. Blue Jays outfielder Joe Carter stepped up to the plate behind the cheers of the home crowd. He slammed a three-run home run off Philadelphia Phillies closer Mitch "Wild Thing" Williams to win Game 6 and the World Series. It was the second time a walk-off home run ended a World Series.

WORST TO FIRST

In 1990 both the Atlanta Braves and Minnesota Twins finished last in their divisions. The Braves ended 65–97, the worst in baseball, and the Twins were 74–88.

The 1991 season turned out to be a different story for both teams. The Braves veteran players, including third baseman Terry Pendleton and outfielder Otis Nixon, had comeback seasons. They also had stellar efforts from young pitchers Steve Avery, John Smoltz, and Tom Glavine. At midseason the Braves were still under .500, but they caught fire in the second half. They squeaked by the Los Angeles Dodgers by one game in the NL West to make the playoffs. With a 94–68 record, they went from worst to first in their division in consecutive seasons.

STEVE AVERY

KENT HRBEK

Meanwhile, the Twins hit their hot streak in June. They won 15 games straight and were fueled by starting pitcher Scott Erickson, who was 12–2 in the season's first half. The offense was led by Kirby Puckett, Kent Hrbek, and Chili Davis. The Twins finished the season on top of the AL West with a 95–67 record—another worst-to-first team. Until that year, no team had gone from worst to first in consecutive seasons.

Things became more interesting in the playoffs. The Braves bested the Pittsburgh Pirates in the National League Championship Series in seven games, and the Twins beat the Toronto Blue Jays in five games. The World Series was set to pit the two underdogs against each other. The 1991 World Series was one of the closest championship series in pro baseball. The Twins won the first two games, but the Braves won the next three and came within one game of winning it all. The Twins won Game 6 to set up the decisive Game 7. The Twins' Jack Morris pitched 10 innings of shutout ball, and Minnesota won it in the bottom of the 10th on a walk-off, game-winning pinch hit by reserve first baseman Gene Larkin.

Dan Gladden is mobbed by his teammates as he scores the winning run of the 1991 World Series.

FACT:

The Cincinnati Reds did the opposite of the Twins and Braves in 1991, going from first to worst. The Reds, who swept the 1990 World Series, finished 1991 at 74–88. It was the worst a World Series championship team had done in its following season.

CHAPTER 5

FAN FAVORITES

RARE PLAYS

THE CYCLE

When a hitter collects at least one single, double, triple, and home run in a game, it's called hitting for the cycle. Even more rare is the "natural cycle"—getting the four hits in order from single to home run. Only 14 players in major league history have hit for the natural cycle.

In 2006 Gary Matthews Jr. became the 14th player to hit for the natural cycle.

THE INSIDE-THE-PARK HOME RUN

One of the most exciting plays in all of baseball is the inside-the-park homer. During this amazing feat, the ball is usually hit hard, but it doesn't go over the fence. The batter has to sprint around the bases in the time it takes the outfielders to get the ball and throw it in. The play often ends in a close play at home plate. Speedy outfielder "Wahoo" Sam Crawford, who played for the Cincinnati Reds and Detroit Tigers from 1899 to 1917, hit an amazing 12 inside-the-park home runs in 1901.

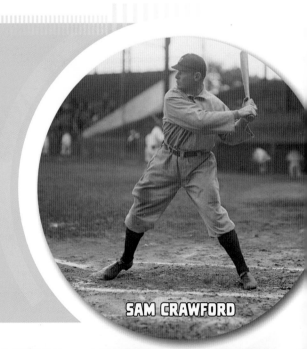

SAM CRAWFORD

THE GRAND SLAM

Things get exciting enough when a team loads the bases. When a batter launches a home run with the bases loaded, fans go wild. Lou Gehrig had the most career grand slams with 23. In 1999 third baseman Fernando Tatis of the St. Louis Cardinals hit two grand slams in the same inning. He is the only major league player to achieve such a feat.

Alex Rodriguez is tied for second with Manny Ramirez behind Lou Gehrig on the all-time list for career grand slams with 21.

THE TRIPLE PLAY

The rare triple play occurs when the defense makes three outs in one continuous play in the same inning. In 1990 the Minnesota Twins became the only team to turn two triple plays in one game. When a single player gets all three outs in an inning during the same play, it's called an unassisted triple play. The play usually happens when two baserunners are on the move during a hit and run. The batter lines out to either the shortstop or second baseman (one out). The fielder then steps on second base (two outs) and then tags the runner coming from first (three outs). This rare play has occurred only 15 times in major league history.

THE PERFECT GAME

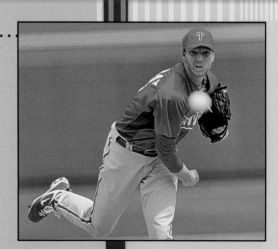

Starting pitchers aren't expected to get every hitter out. But 20 times in major league history, a pitcher has finished a game without allowing a single baserunner to reach base from a hit, walk, error, or hit batsman. Don Larsen of the New York Yankees threw baseball's most famous perfect game versus the Brooklyn Dodgers in Game 5 of the 1956 World Series. Dallas Braden of the Athletics and Roy Halladay of the Philadelphia Phillies completed perfect games in 2010.

Roy Halladay almost earned a second perfect game in 2010. He pitched a no-hitter and walked one batter in a playoff game against the Cincinnati Reds.

THREE STRIKES AND YER OUT!

The art of pitching relies on deception. To keep hitters off balance, pitchers mix it up by throwing fast and slow. They also put spin on the ball to keep the hitters guessing. Here are the most familiar pitches and the pitchers who mastered the art.

FASTBALL

The most basic pitch is the fastball. The pitch can be thrown in many ways, including the split finger, two-seam, or four-seam. Throughout baseball's early history, pitchers such as Walter Johnson, Christy Mathewson, Lefty Grove, and Smoky Joe Wood were known for heating it up. Fireballers such as Bob Feller, Bob Gibson, and Goose Gossage followed, as did flamethrowers Roger Clemens, Dwight Gooden, and Randy Johnson. Nolan Ryan, the major league strikeout leader, was the first pitcher to be recorded at throwing more than 100 miles per hour in a pro game. In 2010 rookie Aroldis Chapman of the Washington Nationals threw the fastest recorded pitch: a 105.1 mile-per-hour inside fastball that was called a ball.

RANDY JOHNSON

CURVEBALL

To complement the straight fastball, early pitchers developed a curveball to deceive the hitters. A curveball is thrown by gripping the ball's seam with the middle finger and snapping the wrist upon release. This motion gives the ball a side-spinning rotation and makes it curve. Mordecai "Three Finger" Brown threw a unique version of the curveball in the early 1900s because of a missing index finger on his pitching hand. Sandy Koufax devastated batters with his bender in the 1950s and 1960s. Bert Blyleven racked up many strikeouts with his roundhouse curve in the 1970s and 1980s. Today Dodgers' Clayton Kershaw and Cardinals' Adam Wainwright fool hitters with their nasty curves.

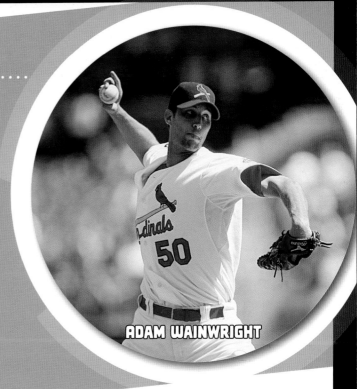

ADAM WAINWRIGHT

JOHAN SANTANA

CHANGEUP

Changing speeds is a technique used to throw off batters' timing. Pitchers throughout history have thrown specialty pitches such as the knuckleball, fadeaway, drop ball, or circle changeup to keep hitters off-balance. Johan Santana of the New York Mets and Roy Halladay of the Philadelphia Phillies have some of the best changeups in the game today.

MIDSUMMER CLASSIC

Since 1933 Major League Baseball has held an All-Star Game about halfway through the season. Also known as the Midsummer Classic, the game was created to give players a break from the long season. It also allows fans to watch the best players of both the AL and NL take the field at the same time.

The 1934 All-Star Game, held at New York's Polo Grounds, produced one of the greatest pitching moments of all time. National League starter Carl Hubbell of the New York Giants took the mound in the first inning. Hubbell, the National League leader in wins (21) and shutouts (10) the previous season, started poorly. He gave up a base hit to Detroit Tigers second baseman Charlie Gehringer. Then he walked Washington Senators outfielder Heinie Manush. Legendary New York Yankees sluggers Babe Ruth and Lou Gehrig were up to bat next. Equally dangerous Jimmie Foxx of the Philadelphia Athletics was in the hole.

American League players from the 1937 All-Star Game (from left): Lou Gehrig, Joe Cronin, Bill Dickey, Joe DiMaggio, Charlie Gehringer, Jimmie Foxx, and Hank Greenberg

As Ruth stepped into the batter's box, Hubbell started spinning his screwball. The Babe went down looking on a called third strike. Gehrig came up next but went down swinging. Foxx, who was warned by Gehrig of Hubbell's nasty screwball, struck out to end the inning. But Hubbell wasn't done. The next inning he struck out White Sox outfielder Al Simmons and Senators shortstop Joe Cronin. Hubbell threw three scoreless innings, but the American League pulled out a 9-7 win. Since then no other pitcher has struck out five future Hall of Famers in a row.

The 2009 MLB All-Star Game in St. Louis, Missouri

FACT:

At the 1984 Major League Baseball All-Star Game in San Francisco, Carl Hubbell was invited to throw out the first pitch. He then watched as National League pitchers Dwight Gooden of the New York Mets and Fernando Valenzuela of the L.A. Dodgers teamed to strike out six consecutive American League All-Stars (including future Hall of Famers Dave Winfield, Reggie Jackson, and George Brett).

BEST NICKNAMES

MR. OCTOBER

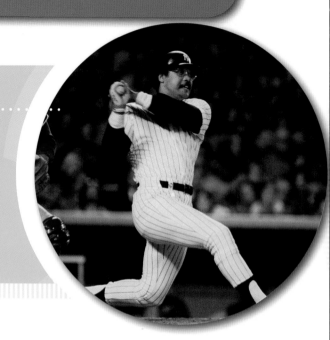

Slugging outfielder Reggie Jackson seemed to save his biggest hits for the postseason in October. He won World Series MVPs with the Oakland A's in 1973 and the New York Yankees in 1977. In the 1977 Series, Jackson walloped three homers in the decisive Game 6.

BONEHEAD

On September 23, 1908, rookie Fred Merkle of the New York Giants earned his nickname by making a terrible baserunning mistake. He didn't touch second base, and the Giants didn't get the run they needed to beat the Chicago Cubs. The game ended in a tie, and the two teams competed in a one-game playoff for a postseason berth. The Cubs won and went on to take the World Series. Though Merkle played 15 more pro seasons, his nickname never left him.

EE-YAH

Hughie Jennings was a shortstop who helped the Baltimore Orioles to National League championships in 1894, 1895, and 1896. He set the major league record for times being hit by a pitch in a season (51) and career (287). He was famous for yelling "ee-yah" and hooting and whistling at fellow players in encouragement.

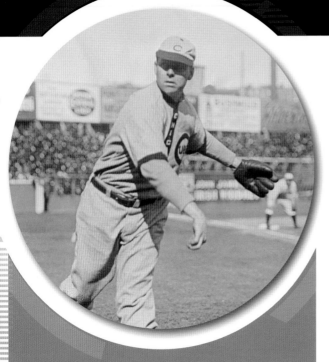

SHOELESS JOE

Joe Jackson was one of the best hitters of the early 20th century. He had a .356 batting average for his career. He was nicknamed "Shoeless" after playing a game in his youth in socks because his cleats hurt his feet. His career came to an abrupt end when he was banned from baseball during his prime. He and his Chicago White Sox teammates were accused of throwing the 1919 World Series and banned for life. Jackson spent the rest of his life insisting he was innocent.

THREE FINGER

Mordecai Brown's right index finger was severed in a farm accident in his Indiana youth. The remaining fingers on his hand were later broken. Though Brown's hand was gnarled, he used his handicap to his advantage by learning to put special spin on the ball. From 1903 to 1916, he won 20 or more games each season in six seasons for the Chicago Cubs.

TRIVIA

Can you match these 10 nicknames to the correct player?

1. Say Hey Kid	Harmon Killebrew
2. The Iron Horse	Frank Thomas
3. The Silver Fox	Lou Gehrig
4. The Flying Dutchman	Honus Wagner
5. Pops	Willie Mays
6. Cool Papa	Joseph Williams
7. Killer	Edwin "Duke" Snider
8. Bye-Bye	Willie Stargell
9. Cyclone	Steve Balboni
10. The Big Hurt	James Bell

Answers: 1. Willie Mays 2. Lou Gehrig 3. Edwin "Duke" Snider 4. Honus Wagner 5. Willie Stargell 6. James Bell 7. Harmon Killebrew 8. Steve Balboni 9. Joseph Williams 10. Frank Thomas

BALLPARKS, PAST AND PRESENT

Since baseball's beginnings, the sport has been labeled America's Pastime. A big reason for that is the appeal of green grass, blue sky, and rich dirt. Here are the best and most beloved Major League Baseball ballparks of all time.

FENWAY PARK

Boston's Fenway Park is Major League Baseball's oldest ballpark still in use. From the famed "Green Monster" left field wall to the hand-operated scoreboard, the Fenway experience relives old-time baseball.

WRIGLEY FIELD

The second-oldest ballpark belongs to the Chicago Cubs. Opened in 1914, it remains a thing of beauty with its ivy-covered outfield walls. Wrigley Field used outdoor lighting to play its first night game in 1988, 74 years after it opened.

ORIOLE PARK AT CAMDEN YARDS

Considered the first "retro park" to be built, the Orioles were on to something when they opened Camden Yards in 1992. With a statue of Baltimore hometowner Babe Ruth and architectural tributes to ballparks past, Camden Yards became the park other new parks emulated.

YANKEE STADIUM

The "House That Ruth Built" was vacated in 2009 for a fancier, updated stadium across the street. However, the old Yankee Stadium that was built in 1923 had unmatched history. Babe Ruth hit the stadium's first home run, and it became home to 26 New York Yankees World Series championship teams.

AT&T PARK

One of the most beautiful modern parks in the major leagues houses the San Francisco Giants. Home run balls hit deep to right splash down in "McCovey Cove"—a spot in the San Francisco Bay unofficially named after famed Giants first baseman Willie McCovey. Outfielder Barry Bonds hit his record-breaking 756th home run at AT&T Park.

SAFECO FIELD

In rainy Seattle the Mariners did the right thing when they built a beautiful stadium with a retractable roof. Opened in 1999, Safeco Field's roof doesn't entirely enclose the stadium, but acts as an umbrella. It can be opened or closed in approximately 15 minutes.

DOWN ON THE FARM

While the baseball spotlight has always been fixed on the major leagues, players in the minor leagues—or farm teams—have had amazing performances as well.

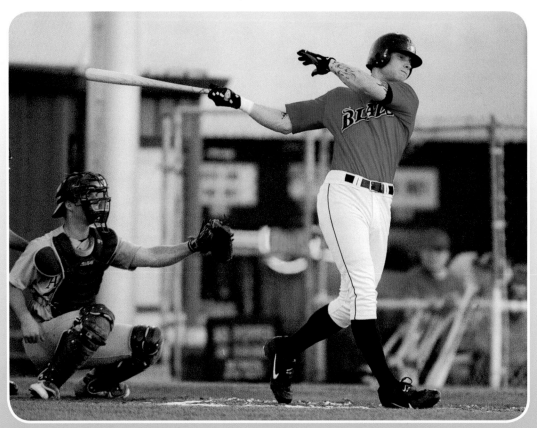

Josh Hamilton takes a swing during a 2002 minor league game.

STRIKE THREE!

On May 13, 1952, 19-year-old pitcher Ron Necciai struck out 27 batters in a single game. Although one batter was retired on a ground ball, Necciai's catcher dropped a third strike and the batter reached first base in the ninth inning. Necciai then struck out the next batter, making it four strikeouts in one inning to finish the game. Necciai made the big leagues with the Pittsburgh Pirates later that season. He went just 1–6 with a 7.08 ERA. He later tore his rotator cuff and never made it back to the majors.

HOLY MOLY!

The Los Angeles Angels of the 1934 Pacific Coast League are regarded as one of the best teams in minor league history. The Angels finished an incredible 137–50. The team featured two stars in the outfield: Frank Demaree and Jigger Statz. Demaree led the PCL in batting average (.383), home runs (45), and RBIs (173). He later played 12 successful seasons in the majors, mostly with the Chicago Cubs. Statz, considered to be one of the greatest minor players, played 18 seasons with the Angels in the PCL and still holds many records.

WHAT AN INNING!

Gene "Half Pint" Rye stood just 5 feet 6 inches (168 centimeters). But in the eighth inning of a Texas League game on August 6, 1930, he must have felt 10 feet tall. His Waco Cubs were trailing the Beaumont Exporters 6-2. That's when Rye stroked three home runs—in the same inning—to lead his club to an 18-run explosion and a 20-7 victory.

FACT:

Minor league baseball teams often have unusual nicknames, including: Lancaster Red Roses, Beaumont Millionaires, San Francisco Seals, Enid Harvesters, Keokuk Kernels, Memphis Chicks, Asheville Tourists, Toledo Mudhens, Lehigh Valley IronPigs, Colorado Springs Sky Sox, Salt Lake Bees, Richmond Flying Squirrels, and Modesto Nuts.

BACK INTO THE SWING

MLB players who spend time on the disabled list might play in minor league games once the injury has healed. After they get back in the rhythm of playing in games and the trainers determine the injury isn't an issue, the players return to the majors.

Melky Cabrera works to get his timing back during a minor league game after being on the disabled list.

MASCOTS

The San Diego Padres introduced The San Diego Chicken as an on-the-field mascot in 1972. Fans, especially the young ones, were impressed, and most of the other major league teams eventually added their own colorful mascots.

Astros—Junction Jack

Athletics—Stomper

Blue Jays—Ace

Braves—Homer and Rally

Brewers—Bernie Brewer and The Sausages

Cardinals—Fredbird

Diamondbacks—Baxter the Bobcat

Giants—Lou Seal

Indians—Slider

Mariners—Mariner Moose

Marlins—Billy the Marlin

Mets—Mr. Met

Nationals—Screech and The Presidents

Orioles—The Bird

Padres—Swinging Friar

Phillies—Phillie Phanatic

Pirates—Pirate Parrot and Captain Jolly Roger

Rangers—Rangers Captain

Rays—Raymond

Reds—Mr. Redlegs, Gapper, and Rosie Red

Red Sox—Lefty and Righty and Wally the Green Monster

Rockies—Dinger the Dinosaur

Royals—Slugerrr

Tigers—Paws

Twins—T. C. Bear

White Sox—Southpaw

FACT:

Only four teams don't have on-the-field mascots: the Angels, Cubs, Dodgers, and Yankees.

TIMELINE

CHRISTY MATHEWSON

REGGIE JACKSON

1876 — The National League begins play with an eight-team league including the league champion Chicago White Stockings

1884 — Charley "Old Hoss" Radbourne of the Providence Grays sets the record for pitching victories in a season with an astonishing 59 wins

1901 — The American League begins play with eight teams: the Baltimore Orioles, Boston Americans, Chicago White Sox, Cleveland Blues, Detroit Tigers, Milwaukee Brewers, Philadelphia Athletics, and Washington Senators

1903 — The first World Series is played, pitting the best American League team against the best National League team; Boston defeats Pittsburgh five games to three

1906 — An All-Chicago World Series occurs when the heavily favored Cubs take on the White Sox; the White Sox upset the Cubs four games to two

1908 — The Chicago Cubs win back-to-back World Series titles, the only World Series titles in their franchise's history

1919 — Chicago "Black Sox" scandal occurs when the Chicago White Sox are accused of throwing the World Series against the Cincinnati Reds

1939 — After playing 2,130 games in a row over 14 years, New York Yankees first baseman Lou Gehrig sits out a game on May 2; he was diagnosed with ALS the following month

1951 — Robby Thompson of the New York Giants hits the "Shot Heard Round the World" for a home run to beat the Brooklyn Dodgers in a game to decide the National League pennant

1961 — Roger Maris hits 61 home runs, breaking Babe Ruth's record for homers in a single season

1968 — In the Year of the Pitcher, Detroit Tigers hurler Denny McLain wins 31 games, the first and only pitcher to win 30 games since Dizzy Dean in 1934

1976 — The Cincinnati Reds win back-to-back World Series championships with a squad known as the Big Red Machine

1985	On September 11, Pete Rose of the Cincinnati Reds slaps hit number 4,192 to break Ty Cobb's major-league record; Rose finishes with 4,256 hits overall before retiring in 1986
1994	Baseball players go on strike and no World Series is played for the first time since 1904
1996	On September 6, Baltimore Orioles shortstop Cal Ripken Jr. breaks Lou Gehrig's consecutive games played streak by playing in his 2,131st game; Ripken extends the streak to 2,632 games before taking a breather in 1998
1997	The Florida Marlins come out of nowhere to take the World Series title in just their fifth year as a franchise by defeating the Cleveland Indians; they do it again against the New York Yankees six years later
2004	The Boston Red Sox win the World Series for the first time in 86 years to break the Curse of the Bambino
2009	The New York Yankees win the World Series, improving their record number of World Series titles to 27
2010	The San Francisco Giants beat the Texas Rangers in the World Series; it is the Giants first championship since 1954

DUSTIN PEDROIA

Match the current MLB team with one of its old names.

Cleveland Indians   Expos

Atlanta Braves   Pilots

Chicago Cubs   Bees

Detroit Tigers   Colts

Minnesota Twins   Gothams

Washington Nationals   Naps

Milwaukee Brewers   Senators

San Francisco Giants   Wolverines

Answer: Indians—Naps; Braves—Bees; Cubs—Colts; Tigers—Wolverines; Twins—Senators; Nationals—Expos; Brewers—Pilots; Giants—Gothams

GLOSSARY

BACKSTOP: another name for a catcher

BATTER'S BOX: area beside the plate designated for the batter; there is a batter's box on either side of home plate, and it measures 6 feet (1.8 m) by 4 feet (1.2 m) in the major leagues

BATTING AVERAGE (BA): number of hits divided by the number of at bats

BULLPEN: all of a team's relief pitchers

CLUTCH: describes a player who performs well during crucial moments of the game

CYCLE: when a player collects a single, double, triple, and home run in a single game

EARNED RUN AVERAGE (ERA): a pitching stat that measures how many runs a pitcher allows every nine innings

HOME RUN (HR): a hit that clears the outfield wall in fair territory

ON DECK CIRCLE: area between the dugout and the batter's box where the next hitter gets ready to bat

RUN BATTED IN (RBI): a batter receives an RBI when he drives in a run

SAVE: statistic awarded to a relief pitcher if he enters a game with his team ahead by three or fewer runs and sucessfully pitches the rest of the game while maintaining a lead

SIGNATURE: describes a move or playing style for which an athlete is best known

WALK-OFF HOME RUN: a home run hit in the bottom of the final inning that gives the home team the winning run

UNANIMOUS: agreed on by everyone

READ MORE

Berman, Len. *The 25 Greatest Baseball Players of All Time.* Naperville, Ill.: Sourcebooks, 2010.

Buckley, James, Jr. *The Child's World Encyclopedia of Baseball.* Mankato, Minn.: Child's World, 2009.

Jacobs, Greg. *The Everything Kids' Baseball Book: Today's Superstars, Great Teams, Legends—and Tips on Playing Like a Pro!* Avon, Mass.: Adams Media, 2006.

Nelson, Kadir. *We Are the Ship: The Story of Negro League Baseball.* New York: Jump at the Sun/Hyperion Books for Children, 2008.

Stout, Glenn. *Baseball Heroes.* Boston, Mass.: Houghton Mifflin Harcourt, 2011.

INTERNET SITES

FactHound offers a safe, fun way to find Internet sites related to this book. All of the sites on FactHound have been researched by our staff.

Here's all you do:

Visit www.facthound.com

Type in this code: 9781429654678

Super-cool stuff!

Check out projects, games and lots more at
www.capstonekids.com

INDEX

POUND RIDGE LIBRARY
271 Westchester Avenue
Pound Ridge, New York
10576-1714